NUMBER AND ALGEBRA

9781420293944
CB138136

CODE CRACKER

In a number and letter code, the word HE equals the number 85.
In the same code, the word BEE equals the number 255.

What do these words equal in the code?

a) DIG

b) EDGE

c) SHARE

Extension

How many years in a 453 145?

Make up more problems like this one. See if a classmate can work them out.

Strategy hints!

1. Look for the important words in the question.
2. Look for a pattern.

ISBN 978 1 4202 9394 4

LETTER SHIFT

In a secret code, letters are changed.
CAT turns into DBU and BULL turns into CVMM.

a) My pet is a GSPH. What is my pet?
b) My sister's name is KFTTJDB. What is her name?
c) My sister is UXFMWF. What does this mean?

Extension

Write a whole sentence in this code. See if a classmate can work it out.

Strategy hints!

1. Look for the important words in the question.
2. Look for a pattern.
9. Think logically.

ISBN 978 1 4202 9394 4

LETTER PATTERN

A, C, E, G . . .

a) What comes next in this letter pattern?

b) What comes in 7th place? What comes in 10th place?

c) How many letters will there be in this pattern? What will the last letter be?

Extension

Make up a letter pattern using different letters of the alphabet. Then, write some problems using this pattern. See if a classmate can work them out.

Strategy hints!

1. Look for the important words in the question.
2. Look for a pattern.
9. Think logically.

ISBN 978 1 4202 9394 4

SYMBOL SHOCKER

2 [*] 3 = 21
4 [*] 3 = 41
5 [*] 0 = 48

a) What does [*] stand for?
b) Find the solution to this problem:
8 [*] 7

Extension

Find the solution to this problem:
3 [*] 3 + 1 [*] 7

Strategy hints!

1 Look for the important words in the question.
2 Look for a pattern.
9 Think logically.

ISBN 978 1 4202 9394 4

READ THE SIGNS

9 [^] 3 [#] 2 = 8
10 [^] 7 [#] 3 = 6

a) What do [^] and [#] stand for?
b) Find the solution to this problem:
45 [^] 18 [#] 13

Extension

Make up some more problems like this one using the symbols [^] and [#]. See if a classmate can work them out.

Strategy hints!

1. Look for the important words in the question.
2. Look for a pattern.
9. Think logically.

ISBN 978 1 4202 9394 4

CALCULATOR SLIP

Professor Digit types 100 into a calculator.
The professor wants to then add 10 and 20 and 5,
but hits a wrong button on the way.
On the screen the professor sees the number 95.

What did the professor type?

Extension

Professor Digit tries to add 10, 20 and 5 to 100.
The answer on the screen is 75. What did the Professor type?

Strategy hints!

1 Look for the important words in the question.

3 Have a go.

9 Think logically.

ISBN 978 1 4202 9394 4

WRONG NUMBER

Professor Digit wants to type [10] [+] [10] [−] [10] [+] [1] into a calculator, but makes a mistake.
The answer on the screen is 91.

What did the professor type?

Extension

Try these problems:

a) [5] [×] [2] [×] [2] [+] [1] Answer on screen = 11

b) [3] [×] [5] [−] [2] [−] [3] Answer on screen = 9

Are these answers correct? What did the professor type?

Strategy hints!

1 Look for the important words in the question.

3 Have a go.

9 Think logically.

ISBN 978 1 4202 9394 4

BOXED IN

Fill in the boxes with the numbers 7, 4, 6 and 5 to make the number sentence true.

$\square \times \square + \square - \square = 19$

Extension

Fill in the boxes with the numbers to make these number sentences true:

a) 2, 8, 5 and 10 $\square - \square \times \square \times \square = 20$

b) 10, 3, 4 and 5 $\square \times \square \times \square - \square = 50$

Is there more than one answer for each question?

Strategy hints!

1 Look for the important words in the question.

3 Have a go.

9 Think logically.

ISBN 978 1 4202 9394 4

BOXED UP

Fill in the boxes with the numbers 3, 5, 0 and 2 to make the number sentence true.

□ □ x □ – □ = 55

See if you can find more than one answer.

Extension

Fill in the boxes with the numbers 2, 5, 7 and 6 to make the number sentence true.

□ □ – □ x □ = 102

Strategy hints!

1. Look for the important words in the question.
3. Have a go.
9. Think logically.

ISBN 978 1 4202 9394 4

COIN COUNT

Benjamin has $1.40.
He counts the money and sees that he has 6 coins.

What might the coins be? See how many different answers you can find.

Extension

Pearl has $1.60. She counts the money and sees that she has 4 coins.

What might the coins be?

Find 3 different answers that work.

Strategy hints!

1 Look for the important words in the question.

3 Have a go.

9 Think logically.

ISBN 978 1 4202 9394 4

LIGHT BAR LOGIC

Type 2 into your calculator.
You will see that it takes 5 light bars to show this number.

Find all the numbers, less than 50, that are made up of 2, 3, 4 or 5 light bars.

Extension

Find all the numbers from 20 to 50 that are made up of 6, 7, 8 or 9 light bars.

Strategy hints!

1 Look for the important words in the question.

9 Think logically.

ISBN 978 1 4202 9394 4

LIGHT LESSON

Type 54 into your calculator.
You will see that it takes 9 light bars to show this number.
Now, type 45 into your calculator.
You will see that it also takes 9 light bars to show this number.

Type 234 and count the light bars. Now find a similar number that uses the same number of light bars. See how many you can find.

Extension

688 uses 20 light bars when it is typed into a calculator. There are 7 other 3-digit numbers that use 20 light bars. Find these numbers.

Strategy hints!

1 Look for the important words in the question.

9 Think logically.

ISBN 978 1 4202 9394 4

LIGHTEN UP

What is the biggest number that uses 7 light bars when it is typed into a calculator? Clue: it is a 2-digit number.

Extension

On a calculator, 7 numbers (one 1-digit number and six 2-digit numbers) are shown by 7 light bars. Find these numbers.

Strategy hints!

1 Look for the important words in the question.

9 Think logically.

ISBN 978 1 4202 9394 4

GIRAFFES AND PANDAS

Giraffes and pandas are sold in a toyshop.
2 giraffes cost $14.
1 giraffe and 1 panda cost $13.

a) How much does 1 giraffe cost?
b) How much does 1 panda cost?

Extension

a) You buy 5 giraffes and 2 pandas. You pay with a $50 note. How much change do you get?

b) For every 5 giraffes you buy in the toyshop, you get 1 for free. How much would 12 giraffes cost?

Strategy hints!

1. Look for the important words in the question.
3. Have a go.
9. Think logically.

ISBN 978 1 4202 9394 4

FOOTBALLS AND CRICKET BATS

In a sports shop, 10 footballs cost $80.
2 cricket bats cost $12.

What is the total cost for 1 football and 1 cricket bat?

Extension

a) How much do 2 footballs and 3 cricket bats cost?

b) How much do 5 footballs and 6 cricket bats cost?

Strategy hints!

1. Look for the important words in the question.
3. Have a go.
9. Think logically.

ISBN 978 1 4202 9394 4

SHOES AND SOCKS

You buy 1 pair of shoes and 1 pair of socks. Together, they cost $40.
The shoes cost 3 times as much as the socks.

How much does 1 pair of socks cost?

Extension

You have $100.

a) Do you have enough money to buy 3 pairs of shoes and 2 pairs of socks?

b) Do you have enough money to buy 2 pairs of shoes and 3 pairs of socks?

Strategy hints!

1 Look for the important words in the question.

3 Have a go.

9 Think logically.

ISBN 978 1 4202 9394 4

HATS AND GLOVES

1 plastic hat and 1 pair of gloves cost $2.
The gloves are 20 cents cheaper than the hat.

How much does 1 pair of gloves cost?

Extension

Make up more problems like this one. See if a classmate can work them out.

Strategy hints!

1. Look for the important words in the question.
3. Have a go.
9. Think logically.

ISBN 978 1 4202 9394 4

GOLDFISH AND SEAHORSES

In a pet shop, 5 goldfish and 1 seahorse cost $25.
Natasha bought 6 goldfish and 1 seahorse for $28.

How much does 1 seahorse cost?

Extension

In the same shop 1 goldfish, 1 seahorse and 1 shell cost $15.

How much does 1 shell cost?

Strategy hints!

1. Look for the important words in the question.
3. Have a go.
9. Think logically.

ISBN 978 1 4202 9394 4

GRAND SALE

The Lowbuy store is having a grand sale.
All items are half price.
Before the sale, books were $10 each and pens were $4 each.

During the sale, how much do 3 books and 2 pens cost?

Extension

a) During the sale, can you buy 5 books and 5 pens if you only have $40?

b) Can you buy 8 books and 7 pens if you only have $50?

Strategy hints!

1 Look for the important words in the question.

3 Have a go.

9 Think logically.

ISBN 978 1 4202 9394 4

WHAT NUMBER AM I?

I am a 3-digit number.
2 of my digits are the same.
My 10s digit uses the highest digit in my number.
My 1s and 100s digits add up to 16.

What number am I?

Extension

Make up some problems like this one. See if a classmate can work them out.

Strategy hints!

1 Look for the important words in the question.
3 Have a go.
9 Think logically.

ISBN 978 1 4202 9394 4

NAME MY NUMBER

I am a 3-digit number.
My digits add up to 10.
My 1s and 100s digits are different by 1.
My 100s digit is shown with 2 light bars on a calculator.

What number am I?

Extension

If my 100s digit is shown with 4 light bars on a calculator, and not 2, what number am I? All the other clues are the same.

Strategy hints!

1 Look for the important words in the question.

3 Have a go.

9 Think logically.

ISBN 978 1 4202 9394 4

NUMBER ME

I am a 3-digit number.
I am in the 5 times table.
I am an odd number.
My digits are in counting order.

What number am I?

Extension

Make up some problems like this one. See if a classmate can work them out.

Strategy hints!

1 Look for the important words in the question.
3 Have a go.
9 Think logically.

ISBN 978 1 4202 9394 4

KNOW MY NUMBER

I am more than 300 but less than 500.
I am an even number.
There is a 7 in my number.
My 100s digit is even.

a) List all of the numbers that I could be.

b) If my 1s digit is bigger than 7, which numbers can I be?

Extension

Make up some problems like this one. See if a classmate can work them out.

Strategy hints!

1. Look for the important words in the question.
3. Have a go.
9. Think logically.

ISBN 978 1 4202 9394 4

NUMBER QUIZ

I am a 3-digit number.
My 3 digits add up to 14.
My 10s digit is my highest digit.
All my digits are even.

What number am I?

Extension

If only my 10s digit is even, what number am I?

Strategy hints!

1 Look for the important words in the question.

3 Have a go.

9 Think logically.

ISBN 978 1 4202 9394 4

INDIA'S MONEY

India has an amount of money.
2 coins have a platypus on them.
1 coin is not round.
2 coins have a mob of kangaroos on them.
The other 3 coins are the same as each other. They are not $2 coins or 10 cent coins.

How much money does India have?

Extension

Make up some money problems like this one. See if a classmate can work them out.

Strategy hints!

1 Look for the important words in the question.
5 Use a drawing.
9 Think logically.

ISBN 978 1 4202 9394 4

ALL IN A LINE

Brian is in line outside his classroom.
The students in the line are in pairs.
Brian sees 10 students in front of him.
Brian sees 4 pairs of students behind him.

How many students are lined up outside the classroom?

Extension

In the playground, Brian notices that the students are all standing in groups.
3 girls are standing together, then 2 boys, then 3 girls and so on. Brian counts 40 students.
How many students are boys and how many are girls?

Strategy hints!

1 Look for the important words in the question.
5 Use a drawing.
8 Make a model.

ISBN 978 1 4202 9394 4

CLASS LINE

Some of the students in class 2B are lined up.
They are lined up boy, girl, boy, girl . . .
Emma is the 3rd girl in the line.
Emma is halfway along the line.

How many students are in the line?

Extension

Now, all the students in class 2B line up. There are 22 students in the class. Emma is the 3rd girl in the line.
How many boys are in line behind Emma?

Strategy hints!

1 Look for the important words in the question.

5 Use a drawing.

8 Make a model.

ISBN 978 1 4202 9394 4

EASTER EGG HUNT

After an Easter egg hunt, 3 children count their eggs.
James has 12 eggs.
Brittany has 13 eggs.
Caitlin has 8 eggs.
The 3 children decide to share them equally.

How many eggs does each child receive?

Extension

Can the children share the eggs equally if:

a) James has 9 eggs, Brittany has 11 eggs and Caitlin has 6 eggs?

b) James has 23 eggs, Brittany has 14 eggs and Caitlin has 29 eggs?

Strategy hints!

1. Look for the important words in the question.
5. Use a drawing.
8. Make a model.

ISBN 978 1 4202 9394 4

ALI, SAM AND BEN

Ali is 8 years old.
Sam is older than Ali, but younger than Ben.
Sam turns 12 on his next birthday.

List the children from oldest to youngest.

Extension

a) Can Ben be 11 years old?

b) Make up some problems like this one. See if a classmate can work them out.

Strategy hints!

1 Look for the important words in the question.

3 Have a go.

9 Think logically.

ISBN 978 1 4202 9394 4

EQUAL STREET

On Equal Street, all the houses are the same.
The front of every house has 4 windows and 1 door.
Claire walks down the street and counts 28 windows.

How many houses has Claire passed?

Extension

Claire is at house number 11. She has counted all the doors and windows. How many more windows than doors has she counted?

Strategy hints!

1. Look for the important words in the question.
2. Look for a pattern.
9. Think logically.

ISBN 978 1 4202 9394 4

FARMER JOE

Farmer Joe has 5 chickens and 2 pigs in every pen on his farm. Farmer Joe visits some of his pens. He counts 10 pigs.

How many pens has Farmer Joe visited?

Extension

a) How many pigs and how many chickens are there in 12 of Farmer Joe's pens?

b) How many are there in 15 pens?

c) How many are there in 20 pens?

Strategy hints!

1 Look for the important words in the question.

2 Look for a pattern.

9 Think logically.

ISBN 978 1 4202 9394 4

HOW MANY NUMBERS?

How many numbers from 100 to 150 are in both the 2 times and the 5 times tables?

Extension

How many numbers from 150 to 750 are in both the 2 times and the 5 times tables?

Strategy hints!

1 Look for the important words in the question.

9 Think logically.

ISBN 978 1 4202 9394 4

STICKER TIME

Sandi puts her stickers into piles.
When they are put into piles of 2, there is 1 left over. When they are put into piles of 5, there is also 1 left over.

What is the smallest possible number of stickers that Sandi can have?

Extension

Rohan has more than 30 but less than 60 stamps.

The number of his stamps is in the 5 times table but is not in the 2 times table.

Rohan has 3 stamps on every page of his album except the last page where there is only 1 stamp. How many stamps are in Rohan's collection?

Strategy hints!

1 Look for the important words in the question.

3 Have a go.

9 Think logically.

ISBN 978 1 4202 9394 4

STRAIGHT AS AN ARROW

Danny fires 4 arrows at this target.
All 4 arrows score points.
Danny scores 27 points.

Where did Danny's arrows land?

Extension

a) Danny's next 4 arrows also score 27 points, but didn't land exactly as before. Where did these arrows land? (Hint: Some arrows may not have hit the target.)

b) Danny scores 10 points with his next 2 arrows. Find 2 ways that he could have made this score.

Strategy hints!

1 Look for the important words in the question.

9 Think logically.

ISBN 978 1 4202 9394 4

TENS AND ONES

Up to 100, there are nine 2-digit numbers whose 10s digit added to the 1s digit equals 10.

Find these 9 numbers.

Extension

Up to 100, there are seven 2-digit numbers whose 1s digit and 10s digit are different by 6.

Find these 7 numbers.

Strategy hints!

1. Look for the important words in the question.
2. Look for a pattern.
9. Think logically.

ISBN 978 1 4202 9394 4

DIGIT SUM

Between 100 and 199 there are 5 numbers whose digits all add up to 15.

Find these 5 numbers.

Extension

Between 200 and 299 there are 6 numbers whose digits all add up to 15. Find these 6 numbers.

Strategy hints!

1. Look for the important words in the question.
2. Look for a pattern.
9. Think logically.

ISBN 978 1 4202 9394 4

ALL THE TWOS

Rachael writes down all of the numbers from 1 to 100.

How many times does she write '2'?
A table like this might help:

	1 to 19	20 to 29	30 to 100
Number of 2s			

Extension

How many numbers from 199 to 301 will have at least one 2 in them?

Strategy hints!

1. Look for the important words in the question.
2. Look for a pattern.
4. Use a table or a chart.

ISBN 978 1 4202 9394 4

ALL THE DIGITS

Montana writes down all of the numbers from 1 to 100.

How many digits does she write?
A table like this might help:

Range of numbers	1-digit numbers	2-digit numbers	3-digit numbers
Number of digits used			

Extension

If Montana writes down all of the numbers from 100 to 199, how many digits will she write?

Strategy hints!

1. Look for the important words in the question.
2. Look for a pattern.
4. Use a table or a chart.

ISBN 978 1 4202 9394 4

SLIPPERY STAIRS

A frog hops up 5 steps and then slips down 3.
It then hops up 6 steps and slips down 2.
It is now on the 20th step of the stairs.

Which step did the frog start on?

Extension

Make up some problems like this one. See if a classmate can work them out.

Strategy hints!

1 Look for the important words in the question.

5 Use a drawing.

6 Work backwards.

ISBN 978 1 4202 9394 4

SNAKES AND ADDERS

In a game of snakes and ladders, Josh moves up 10 squares.
Next, he moves up 8 squares.
Then, he lands on a snake and falls down 20 squares.
He finishes at number 37.

Which square did Josh start on?

Extension

Josh is at 93 on the board and it is his turn to roll the 2 dice.

What 6 possible rolls will help Josh reach 100 and win the game?

Strategy hints!

1 Look for the important words in the question.

6 Work backwards.

ISBN 978 1 4202 9394 4

GOING HALVES

Milo gives half of his money to Greg. Greg now has $40.
Milo then gives half of the money he has left to Lisa.

How much money does Milo give Lisa?

Extension

Make up some problems like this one. See if a classmate can work them out.

Strategy hints!

1 Look for the important words in the question.

6 Work backwards.

ISBN 978 1 4202 9394 4

WHICH COLUMN?

Numbers are in certain columns in a chart.

A	B	C	D	E	F	G
			1		2	
3		4		5		6
	7		8		9	
10		11		12		13

In which column will the number 20 be written?

Extension

One of the columns has a counting or tables pattern in it.
Which is that column?

Strategy hints!

1. Look for the important words in the question.
2. Look for a pattern.
4. Use a table or a chart.

ISBN 978 1 4202 9394 4

COUNTING COLUMNS

Numbers are in certain columns in a chart.

A	B	C	D	E	F	G	H	I
9	10	11	12	13	14	15	16	17
18	19	20	21	22	23	24	25	26
27	28	29	30	31	32	33	34	35

One of the columns has a counting or tables pattern in it.

Which is that column?

Strategy hints!

1. Look for the important words in the question.
2. Look for a pattern.
4. Use a table or a chart.

Extension

In which column will the number 100 be written?

ISBN 978 1 4202 9394 4

ODD ONE OUT

27, 45, 63, 35, 81

a) Which number is the odd one out?
b) Why is this number the odd one out?

Extension

41, 17, 6, 24, 0

Think about the way these numbers are shown on a calculator. Which number is the odd one out?

Strategy hints!

1. Look for the important words in the question.
2. Look for a pattern.

ISBN 978 1 4202 9394 4

NOT LIKE THE OTHERS

731, 852, 965, 479, 832

a) Which of these numbers is the odd one out?
b) Why is this number the odd one out?

Extension

128, 506, 714, 902, 1145

Which of these numbers is the odd one out?

Strategy hints!

1. Look for the important words in the question.
2. Look for a pattern.

ISBN 978 1 4202 9394 4

ALL THE COINS

You have 1 of every silver coin.
You swap them for the cheapest gold coin.

Do you have more or less money after you swap? How much more, or how much less?

Extension

You now have 1 of every coin.
How much more money do you need to make $5?

Strategy hints!

1 Look for the important words in the question.

ISBN 978 1 4202 9394 4

MAGIC SQUARE

Finish the magic square.
You must use all of the even numbers from 2 to 18.
All of the lines must add up to 30.

16		12
6	10	
	18	

Extension

Make up another magic square that works like this one. Use all of the even numbers from 2 to 18. Each line must add up to 30.

Strategy hints!

1. Look for the important words in the question.
2. Look for a pattern.

ISBN 978 1 4202 9394 4

ALL ABOUT THE PLACE

With the digits 4, 2 and 7 you can make 6 different 3-digit numbers.

List them in order from smallest to biggest.

Extension

Find all the 3-digit numbers that can be made by using the digits 8, 3 and 5.
List them in order from smallest to biggest.

Strategy hints!

1. Look for the important words in the question.
2. Look for a pattern.

ISBN 978 1 4202 9394 4

PERFECT PLACEMENT

With the digits 4, 2 and 4 you can make 3 different 3-digit numbers.

Put them in order from smallest to biggest.

Extension

a) With the digits 4, 2, 2 and 4, you can make 6 different 3-digit numbers. Put them in order from smallest to biggest.

b) Find all the different 4-digit numbers you can make by using the digits 4, 6, 6 and 4.

Strategy hints!

1. Look for the important words in the question.
2. Look for a pattern.

ISBN 978 1 4202 9394 4

MAKING NUMBERS

Katy has the digits 1, 3, 5 and 6. She uses them to make a 4-digit number.

- The number is an odd number. The 10s digit has the highest value.
- The 1000s digit minus the 1s digit equals 2.
- The 10s digit minus the 1000s digit equals the 100s digit.

What number has Katy made?

Extension

Katy has the digits 2, 3, 6 and 9. She uses them to make a 4-digit number.

- If you multiply the 10s digit by itself, you find the 100s digit.
- If you multiply the 1000s digit by the 10s digit, you find the 1s digit.

What number has Katy made?

Strategy hints!

1 Look for the important words in the question.

9 Think logically.

ISBN 978 1 4202 9394 4

MY TOWN

Follow the clues to find the population of my town.

- The population is a 4-digit number.
- The number uses the digits 4, 5, 9 and 9, but not in that order.
- The 10s digit is bigger than the 1000s digit.
- One of the 9s is 100 times bigger than the other 9.

Extension

Make up some problems like this one. See if a classmate can work them out.

Strategy hints!

1 Look for the important words in the question.

9 Think logically.

ISBN 978 1 4202 9394 4

LETTERBOXES

On one side of my street the house numbers are odd numbers.
On the other side of my street the house numbers are even numbers.
My house number is 27.

How many houses, on my side of the street, come before my house?

Extension

There are 61 houses in my street altogether.
How many houses are on the even side of the street?

Strategy hints!

1. Look for the important words in the question.
2. Look for a pattern.

ISBN 978 1 4202 9394 4

STREET KNOWLEDGE

On one side of my street the house numbers are odd numbers.
On the other side of my street the house numbers are even numbers.
My house number, when added to the house number across the street, equals 81.

What are the 2 possible numbers of my house?

Extension

The last house in my street is number 51.
How many houses come after my house, on my side of the street?

Strategy hints!

1. Look for the important words in the question.
2. Look for a pattern.

ISBN 978 1 4202 9394 4

LETTER SALE

At the hardware shop you can buy letters.
The 5 vowels cost $2 each.
The consonants cost $5 each.
My name is Peter. It costs $19 to buy the letters in my name.

Vowels: A E I O U
Consonants: B C D F G H J K L M N P Q R S T V W X Y Z

a) How much does your name cost?
b) How much does a classmate's name cost?
c) How much does your teacher's surname cost?

Extension

a) Find a name that costs $12 at the hardware shop.
b) Find a name that costs $20 at the hardware shop.
c) Find a name that costs $24 at the hardware shop.

Strategy hints!

1. Look for the important words in the question.
2. Look for a pattern.

ISBN 978 1 4202 9394 4

SIGN SALE

At the hardware shop you can buy letters.
The 5 vowels cost $2 each.
The consonants cost $5 each.
SYDNEY costs $27.

Vowels: A E I O U
Consonants: B C D F G H J K L M N P Q R S T V W X Y Z

Write down the town, suburb or city in which you live. How much would it cost to buy the letters to make a sign for this name?

Extension

How many vowels and how many consonants are in the sign if:

a) The letters cost $26? **b)** 8 letters cost $31?

Strategy hints!

1 Look for the important words in the question.
2 Look for a pattern.
9 Think logically.

ISBN 978 1 4202 9394 4

BACK TO BACK

Numbers that are next to each other, like 4 and 5, are called consecutive numbers.

Which 3 consecutive numbers add up to 18?

Extension

Which 3 consecutive numbers add up to:

a) 36?

b) 90?

Strategy hints!

1 Look for the important words in the question.

3 Have a go.

9 Think logically.

ISBN 978 1 4202 9394 4

CONSECUTIVE CHALLENGE

Numbers that are next to each other, like 4 and 5, are called consecutive numbers.

What is the biggest of 3 consecutive numbers that add up to 27?

Extension

What is the smallest of 3 consecutive numbers that add up to:

a) 63?

b) 60?

Strategy hints!

1 Look for the important words in the question.

3 Have a go.

9 Think logically.

ISBN 978 1 4202 9394 4

TEMPERATURE TIMES

In the morning it was 4 degrees.
In the afternoon it rose to 27 degrees.
When I went to bed it was 21 degrees.

By how many degrees did the weather change during the day?

Extension

On another day, the temperature changed by 40 degrees.
In the morning it was 4 degrees. In the afternoon it rose to 26 degrees.
What temperature did it then drop to at night?

Strategy hints!

1 Look for the important words in the question.

5 Use a drawing.

ISBN 978 1 4202 9394 4

ALL SORTS OF SUMS

The number 2012 can be made into many different sums. For example:

2 + 0 + 12 = 14

20 − 1 − 2 = 17

Use the digits in 2012 to make up sums that equal:

a) 32

b) 8

Extension

Now, use the digits in 2012 to make up sums that equal:

a) 3

b) 21

Strategy hints!

1 Look for the important words in the question.

3 Have a go.

9 Think logically.

ISBN 978 1 4202 9394 4

EQUAL COINS

2 echidnas equal 1 lyrebird.
2 lyrebirds equal 1 platypus.
5 platypuses equal 1 mob of kangaroos.

How many echidnas equal 1 mob of kangaroos?

Extension

a) How many lyrebirds equal 1 emu and kangaroo?

b) Make up some problems like this one using coins and notes. See if a classmate can work them out.

Strategy hints!

1 Look for the important words in the question.

5 Use a drawing.

9 Think logically.

ISBN 978 1 4202 9394 4

SO MANY SUMS

The numbers 2, 3 and 5 can be used to make interesting sums. For example:

35 + 2 = 37

2 + 5 − 3 = 4

Make up sums using 2, 3 and 5 that equal:

a) 28

b) 10

Extension

Make up sums using 2, 3 and 5 that equal:

a) 51

b) 22

Strategy hints!

1 Look for the important words in the question.

3 Have a go.

9 Think logically.

ISBN 978 1 4202 9394 4

IN A BRACKET

When a number is outside a bracket, it means lots of or groups of.

2 (4) means 2 groups of 4, which equals 8.

5 (2 + 4) means 5 groups of 6, which equals 30.

Find the answers to these problems:

a) 5 (10)

b) 4 (2 + 4)

c) 10 (9 – 3)

Extension

Make up problems like these that equal 20 and 100.

Strategy hints!

1 Look for the important words in the question.

3 Have a go.

9 Think logically.

ISBN 978 1 4202 9394 4

MICE AND MEN

Solve this mice and men riddle.
My heads are 10.
My mice are 5.
My men the same.

How many legs on my mice and men?

Extension

Make up a riddle like this using ants and cats. See if a classmate can work it out.

Strategy hints!

1 Look for the important words in the question.

5 Use a drawing.

9 Think logically.

ISBN 978 1 4202 9394 4

BICYCLES AND TRICYCLES

Bicycles have 2 wheels.
Tricycles have 3 wheels.
Amelia sees 11 cycles and counts 25 wheels.

How many tricycles does Amelia see?

Extension

Make up a riddle like this using cars and bicycles. See if a classmate can work it out.

Strategy hints!

1 Look for the important words in the question.

5 Use a drawing.

9 Think logically.

ISBN 978 1 4202 9394 4

BIRTHDAY MONEY

Richard makes a special deal for his baby niece Meg.
When Meg turns 1 her present is $1.
When Meg turns 2 her present is $2.
When Meg turns 3 her present is $4 and so on.
On her next birthday, Meg will turn 6.

How much will she be given by Richard?

Extension

a) On which birthday will Meg be given more than $200?

b) How much money will Meg be given on her 10th birthday?

Strategy hints!

1 Look for the important words in the question.

4 Use a table or a chart.

9 Think logically.

ISBN 978 1 4202 9394 4

AUSSIE RULES

In Australian Rules football a goal is worth 6 points and a behind is worth 1 point.
A score of 2 goals and 3 behinds is 6 + 6 + 3 = 15 points.
Madison's team scored 20 points in their game.

How many goals and how many behinds did they score? See how many different answers you can find.

Extension

In their next game, Madison's team scored 27 points. They kicked more goals than behinds. How many goals and how many behinds did they score?

Strategy hints!

1 Look for the important words in the question.
4 Use a table or a chart.
9 Think logically.

ISBN 978 1 4202 9394 4

RUGBY RULES

In Rugby League a try is worth 4 points and a penalty is worth 2 points.
A score of 3 tries and 1 penalty is 4 + 4 + 4 + 2 = 14 points.
Tom's team scored 10 points in their last game.

How many tries and how many penalties did they score? See how many different answers you can find.

Extension

In their next game, Tom's team scored 30 points. The team scored an equal number of tries and penalties. How many tries and how many penalties did they score?

Strategy hints!

1. Look for the important words in the question.
4. Use a table or a chart.
9. Think logically.

ISBN 978 1 4202 9394 4

FOLLOW THE SYMBOLS

The symbol @ means add on 2.
The symbol ^ means double.
The symbol * means take away 4.
Start at 14.
Then * ^ ^ @ *

What number are you on now?

Extension

After you ^ * * @ you are at the number 34.
Where did you start?

Strategy hints!

1 Look for the important words in the question.
6 Work backwards.
9 Think logically.

ISBN 978 1 4202 9394 4

BIGGEST NUMBER

a) 4 numbers add up to 30.
1 of the numbers is 12.
1 of the numbers is 5.
What do the other 2 numbers add up to?

b) 5 numbers add up to 100.
3 of the numbers are 20, 30 and 11.
What is the biggest whole number that 1 of the other numbers can be?

Extension

5 numbers add up to 100.
3 of the numbers are the same and 2 of the numbers are the same.
1 of the numbers is 35.
What are the other 4 numbers?

Strategy hints!

1 Look for the important words in the question.
6 Work backwards.
9 Think logically.

ISBN 978 1 4202 9394 4

Focus Number and place value
- Subtraction

Number and Algebra 70

LEFTOVERS

4 numbers are taken away from 100.
70 is left over.
1 of the numbers is 11.
1 of the numbers is 8.

What do the other 2 numbers add up to?

Extension

5 numbers are taken away from 100.
0 is left over. 2 of the numbers are 20 and 22.

What is the biggest whole number that 1 of the other numbers can be?

Strategy hints!

1 Look for the important words in the question.

6 Work backwards.

9 Think logically.

ISBN 978 1 4202 9394 4

ED AND EVIE

Ed and Evie are brother and sister.
Together, their ages add up to 32.
Ed is 4 years younger than Evie.

How old is Evie?

Extension

Ed has a twin called Eric and Evie has a twin called Emma.
How far are the ages of the 4 children away from 100 years?

Strategy hints!

1. Look for the important words in the question.
3. Have a go.

ISBN 978 1 4202 9394 4

NANNY AND GRANDAD

Nanny is 5 years younger than Grandad.
Next birthday, Grandad will be 71.

How old are Nanny and Grandad altogether?

Extension

When you add up the 4 digits of the year in which Nanny was born, you get my big sister's age. She is 19. Nanny was born before 1950 and after 1936. When was Nanny born?

Strategy hints!

1 Look for the important words in the question.

3 Have a go.

9 Think logically.

ISBN 978 1 4202 9394 4

LUCY AND LOU

Lucy never tells the truth.

Lucy says Lou never tells the truth.

Lou says, “I am double digits years old.”

Lucy says to Lou, “You are an even number of years old.”

What is the youngest age Lou could be?

Extension

Make up a problem like this one. See if a classmate can work it out.

Strategy hints!

1 Look for the important words in the question.

9 Think logically.

ISBN 978 1 4202 9394 4

PLANET ZEBKO

Planet Zebko has its own counting system.

Earth	1	2	3	4	5	6	7	8	9	10
Zebko	(	((	(((	((((	▽	▽(	▽((	▽(((	▽((((	▽▽

On Zebko they never use a symbol more than 4 times.

On Zebko the next new symbol comes at 25 and it looks like this: ↲

What are these numbers?

a) ▽▽▽((

b) ▽▽▽(

c) ↲↲▽(

Extension

When will the Zebko people start using their next new symbol?

Strategy hints!

1 Look for the important words in the question.

2 Look for a pattern.

4 Use a table or a chart.

ISBN 978 1 4202 9394 4

ALIEN MATHS TEST

Planet Zebko has its own counting system.

Earth	1	2	3	4	5	6	7	8	9	10
Zebko	(	((	(((	((((	∇	∇(	∇((	∇(((	∇((((	∇∇

On Zebko they never use a symbol more than 4 times.

On Zebko the next new symbol comes at 25 and it looks like this: ↲

You are at school on Zebko and you have a maths test.

Answer these problems. You can answer in Earth numbers.

a) ∇((+ ∇∇∇

b) ∇∇∇∇ – ∇(

c) ↲↲ x ((

Extension

Make up more Zebko problems. See if a classmate can work them out.

Strategy hints!

1. Look for the important words in the question.
2. Look for a pattern.
4. Use a table or a chart.

ISBN 978 1 4202 9394 4

10 TIMES SMALLER

The king decides that every number must become 10 times smaller.
30 now equals 3 and 600 now equals 60.
Find the answer to:

200 + 40 − 30 + 20 = ?

Extension

a) What will 10 become?

b) What will 5 become?

c) What will 1 become?

Strategy hints!

1 Look for the important words in the question.

2 Look for a pattern.

9 Think logically.

ISBN 978 1 4202 9394 4

PICK THE PATTERN

8, 4, 2, 1 . . .

a) What is happening in this pattern?
b) What comes before 8 in this pattern?
c) What 2 numbers come after 1 in this pattern?
d) What comes next?

Extension

Use this type of pattern.

Start at 256.

How many more numbers will be in this pattern before you reach 1?

Strategy hints!

1 Look for the important words in the question.

2 Look for a pattern.

9 Think logically.

ISBN 978 1 4202 9394 4

JACK, QUEEN, KING

In a card game you use only jacks, queens and kings.
There are 4 jacks, 4 queens and 4 kings.
The jacks are worth 1 point, the queens are worth 2 points and the kings are worth 3 points.
Kumar has 5 cards worth 10 points.

What cards can Kumar have? See how many different answers you can find.

Extension

Kumar has 1 jack, 2 queens and some kings in his hand. Kumar's hand is worth 17 points. How many kings does Kumar have?

Strategy hints!

1. Look for the important words in the question.
2. Look for a pattern.
3. Have a go.

ISBN 978 1 4202 9394 4

ABBEY, BERT AND CINDI

There are 3 students called Abbey, Bert and Cindi.
Their teacher asks them to line up behind each other.

Find all the different ways the students can line up.

Extension

Choose 4 students' names from your class and find out how many ways they can line up.

Strategy hints!

1. Look for the important words in the question.
2. Look for a pattern.
8. Make a model.

ISBN 978 1 4202 9394 4

DOORS AND WINDOWS

New houses are in a street.
They all have 1 window and 1 door at the front that needs painting.
The painter has red and yellow paint. He wants to make each house look different.
He paints the first house's window red and its door yellow.

Figure out all the different ways he can paint the houses. You could use a table to help you.

Extension

If the painter had red, yellow and green paint, figure out all the different ways he could paint the houses in the street.

Strategy hints!

1 Look for the important words in the question.
2 Look for a pattern.
4 Use a table or a chart.

ISBN 978 1 4202 9394 4

FINALS TIME

At the end of the season, the top 4 teams in Ryan's basketball competition are the Jets, the Cheetahs, the Kings and the Doves.
They will now play each other to see who will win the premiership.
All the teams must play each other once.

Figure out how many rounds of matches will be in the finals.
You could use a table to help you.

Extension

The Jets win all of their games. What is the largest number of games that any of the other 3 teams can win?

Strategy hints!

1 Look for the important words in the question.
2 Look for a pattern.
4 Use a table or a chart.

ISBN 978 1 4202 9394 4

PALINDROME PUZZLE

A palindrome is a number or word that is the same forwards and backwards.
464 and LEVEL are examples of palindromes.

Find these number palindromes:

a) The smallest that has 2 digits.

b) The biggest that has 2 digits.

c) The smallest that has 3 digits.

d) The biggest that has 3 digits.

Extension

Find these number palindromes:

a) The 2nd smallest that has 3 digits.

b) The 2nd biggest that has 3 digits.

c) All 3-digit palindromic numbers, bigger than 300, that have a 2 in them.

d) All 3-digit palindromic numbers that have two 2s in them.

Strategy hints!

1. Look for the important words in the question.
2. Look for a pattern.

ISBN 978 1 4202 9394 4

BACK TO FRONT

A palindrome is a number or word that is the same forwards and backwards.
747 and MUM are examples of palindromes.
99 can be made by adding together pairs of palindromes.
11 and 88 is one way of doing this.

Find the other 3 ways.

Extension

121 can be made by adding together pairs of palindromes.
Find all 4 pairs of palindromes that add up to 121.

Strategy hints!

1. Look for the important words in the question.
2. Look for a pattern.

ISBN 978 1 4202 9394 4

TIME IS MONEY

Kensani is paid $2 for every 15 minutes she works.
Kensani works from 11:00 to 12:00 and then from 1:30 to 2:00.

How much money is she paid?

Extension

a) Kensani starts work at 3:00. She wants to earn $14. What time will she stop working?

b) Kensani starts work at 8:00. She works until 12:00, then has a 30 minute break, then works until 2:00. How far off is she from earning $50?

Strategy hints!

1 Look for the important words in the question.

4 Use a table or a chart.

ISBN 978 1 4202 9394 4

NOT 2 OR 5

How many numbers less than 20 are not in either the 2 times table or the 5 times table?

Extension

How many numbers less than 50 are not in either the 2 times table or the 5 times table?

Strategy hints!

1. Look for the important words in the question.
2. Look for a pattern.

ISBN 978 1 4202 9394 4

SHOPPING

I go shopping and I buy:
2 books for $7 each
3 drinks for $4 each
1 sandwich for $5
When I come home I still have $7 in my purse.

How much money was in my purse when I started shopping?

Extension

Make up a shopping story problem like this one. See if a classmate can work it out.

Strategy hints!

1 Look for the important words in the question.

6 Work backwards.

ISBN 978 1 4202 9394 4

2 AWAY

3 numbers are in a line.
They increase by 2 along the line.
The numbers add up to 30.

What are the 3 numbers?

Extension

3 numbers are in a line.
They increase by 2 along the line.
The numbers add up to 66.
What are the 3 numbers?

Strategy hints!

1. Look for the important words in the question.
3. Have a go.
9. Think logically.

ISBN 978 1 4202 9394 4

OUR TOWNS

Meg lives in the town of Ghost Gum.
I live in the town of Fern Creek.
The 2 towns are 36 kilometres away from each other.
Halfway from my town to Ghost Gum there is a petrol station.

How far from Fern Creek is the petrol station?

Extension

Halfway from my town to the petrol station is a waterfall.
How far from Meg's house is the waterfall?

Strategy hints!

1. Look for the important words in the question.
3. Have a go.
5. Use a drawing.

ISBN 978 1 4202 9394 4

COUNTING IN FIVES

Shan starts at 3 and skip counts by 5s.

Which of these numbers will Shan eventually say?
25, 40, 53, 78, 170, 295, 418

Extension

What are the last two 3-digit numbers that Shan will say?

Strategy hints!

1 Look for the important words in the question.

2 Look for a pattern.

ISBN 978 1 4202 9394 4

RACE PLACE

In the final of the boys' sprint, 3 boys finished in front of me.
Joe finished 2 places behind me.
Sam finished last, 4 places behind Joe.

How many boys were in the race?

Extension

The next race was between Amy, Beth, Clare, Danni, Eve and Fiona.
Eve came in front of 4 girls.
The position that Danni came in the race is the same as the position of the first letter of her name in the alphabet.
2 girls finished between Clare and Danni.
Fiona finished one place in front of Beth.
Figure out where each girl finished in the race.

Strategy hints!

1 Look for the important words in the question.
5 Use a drawing.
8 Make a model.

ISBN 978 1 4202 9394 4

MAKE THAT NUMBER

By using the numbers 1, 2, 3, 4 and 5, in that order, you can make lots of different sums that equal lots of different numbers.

Here are some examples:

15 = 1 + 2 + 3 + 4 + 5

7 = 1 + 2 + 3 − 4 + 5

60 = 12 + 3 + 45

Using the numbers 1, 2, 3, 4 and 5, make sums that equal:

a) 5

b) 10

Extension

Using the same numbers, make sums that equal:

a) 23 b) 45

Strategy hints!

1 Look for the important words in the question.

9 Think logically.

ISBN 978 1 4202 9394 4

MARBLES

Grace and Tate share out a bag of 12 marbles.
Grace takes $\frac{1}{3}$ of the marbles.
Tate takes $\frac{1}{4}$ of the marbles.

a) How many marbles do the children get each?
b) How many marbles are left over?

Extension

Grace takes $\frac{1}{3}$ of the marbles. If she takes 12 marbles, how many were in the bag to begin with?

Strategy hints!

1. Look for the important words in the question.
5. Use a drawing.

ISBN 978 1 4202 9394 4

CALCULATOR CORRECTION

Charlie wants to find out the answer to 7 x 2. He uses his calculator.
Charlie makes a mistake and types [7] [+] [2] [=]

a) How far away is the answer on the screen from the answer that he wants?
b) What must Charlie now type into the calculator to find the correct answer?

Extension

What must Charlie type into the calculator to find the correct answer, if:

a) Charlie wants to find 16 ÷ 2. He incorrectly types in [16] [−] [2] [=].

b) Charlie wants to find 12 x 4 + 20. He incorrectly types in [12] [÷] [4] [+] [10] [=].

Strategy hints!

1 Look for the important words in the question.

9 Think logically.

ISBN 978 1 4202 9394 4

AN OPEN BOOK

Michael is reading his new book.
He is in the middle of the book.
There are 124 pages in the book.

Which 2 pages is Michael's book open to?

Extension

One quarter of the pages in Michael's book have pictures.
How many pages of the book have only writing on them?

Strategy hints!

1 Look for the important words in the question.

7 Try an easier problem.

8 Make a model.

ISBN 978 1 4202 9394 4

BOOKED OUT

Andre opens his book.
He adds up the 2 page numbers.

Will the answer be an odd number or an even number?

Extension

Andre opens up a magazine to page 16.
This is halfway to half the number of pages in the magazine.
How many pages are in the magazine?

Strategy hints!

1. Look for the important words in the question.
7. Try an easier problem.
8. Make a model.

ISBN 978 1 4202 9394 4

ANIMAL SIZES

A mouse is $\frac{1}{2}$ as big as a hamster.
A hamster is $\frac{1}{2}$ as big as a rabbit.
A rabbit is $\frac{1}{2}$ as big as a cat.

How many mice are the same size as a cat?

Strategy hints!

1. Look for the important words in the question.
5. Use a drawing.
9. Think logically.

Extension

What fraction of a cat is a mouse?

ISBN 978 1 4202 9394 4

ODD OR EVEN

10 can be shown as 1 + 0 = 1 (an odd number)
26 can be shown as 2 + 6 = 8 (an even number)
From 10 to 30 there are twenty-one 2-digit numbers.

How many of these 21 numbers add up to an even number?

Extension

a) How many numbers from 50 to 70 will be odd when their digits are added up?

b) How many numbers from 99 to 121 will be odd when their digits are added up?

c) How many numbers from 120 to 140 will be even when their digits are added up?

Strategy hints!

1. Look for the important words in the question.
2. Look for a pattern.

ISBN 978 1 4202 9394 4

BUYING STAMPS

Hannah bought some 3 cent stamps and some 5 cent stamps.
Hannah bought 12 stamps.
They cost Hannah 40 cents in total.

How many 3 cent stamps did Hannah buy?

Extension

Hannah also bought some 10 cent stamps and some 25 cent stamps. She bought an equal number of each stamp and the total cost was $2.10.

How many of each stamp did Hannah buy?

Strategy hints!

1. Look for the important words in the question.
3. Have a go.

ISBN 978 1 4202 9394 4

STARTING NUMBER

A number has 5 added to it and then it has 2 taken away.
It is now equal to twice 12.

What was the starting number?

Extension

A number is doubled and then 4 is taken away from it.
The answer is 5 more than the starting number.
What was the starting number?

Strategy hints!

1. Look for the important words in the question.
3. Have a go.
9. Think logically.

ISBN 978 1 4202 9394 4

TENNIS ANYONE?

Alice, Beth, Casey and Danni play tennis.
You need 4 players to play doubles.

Find all the different teams the 4 girls can make to play a doubles match.

Extension

Find all the different singles matches the girls can play without anyone playing the same person twice.

Strategy hints!

1 Look for the important words in the question.
5 Use a drawing.
8 Make a model.

ISBN 978 1 4202 9394 4

MEASUREMENT AND GEOMETRY

THE BEAR FAMILY

1 papa bear weighs the same as 3 baby bears.
2 papa bears weigh the same as 3 mamma bears.

How many baby bears weigh the same as 1 mamma bear?

Extension

Papa bear and mamma bear are on the same side of a seesaw.

How many baby bears are needed on the other side of the seesaw to balance them?

Strategy hints!

1. Look for the important words in the question.
5. Use a drawing.
9. Think logically.

ISBN 978 1 4202 9394 4

SUM

In this grid, the letters S U M must appear in every horizontal and vertical line. They do not need to be in that order.

Finish the grid.

S		
	U	
		M

Strategy hints!

1. Look for the important words in the question.
3. Have a go.
5. Use a drawing.

Extension

Create the same kind of grid with the letters T E N.

ISBN 978 1 4202 9394 4

FILL IN THE SPACE

This is part of a shape made out of rectangles.

The whole shape is also a rectangle.

Some pieces are missing.

How many pieces are missing?

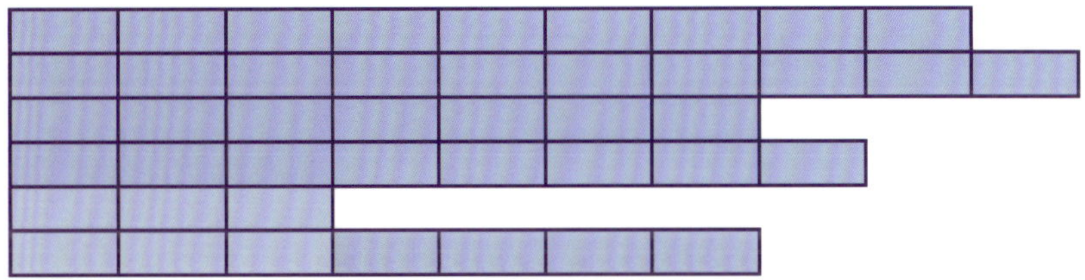

Extension

The rectangle has now been completed.

You decide to colour each individual rectangle of the full shape. No rectangles that touch on an edge can have the same colour.

What is the fewest number of colours you can use?

Strategy hints!

1 Look for the important words in the question.

5 Use a drawing.

9 Think logically.

ISBN 978 1 4202 9394 4

AMAZING DATE

On 23 July 2030 the date will be written as 23/7/30.
This is an addition date.

Find the 5 addition dates in 2030 that will come after this date.

Extension

What is the last addition date before the year 2100?

Strategy hints!

1 Look for the important words in the question.

9 Think logically.

ISBN 978 1 4202 9394 4

ALL THE SQUARES

How many squares can you see in the picture?

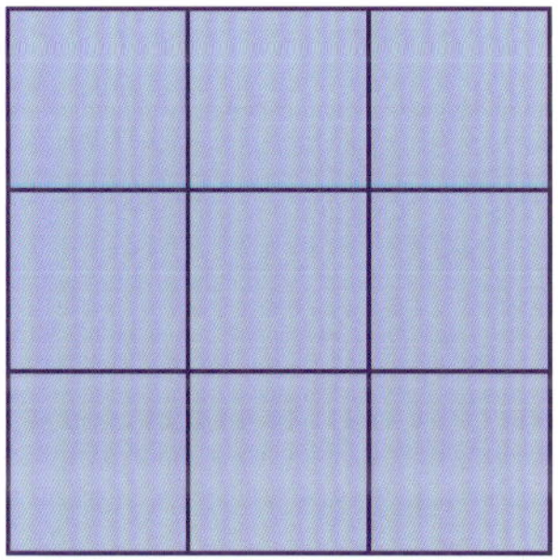

Extension

How many squares can you see in the picture?

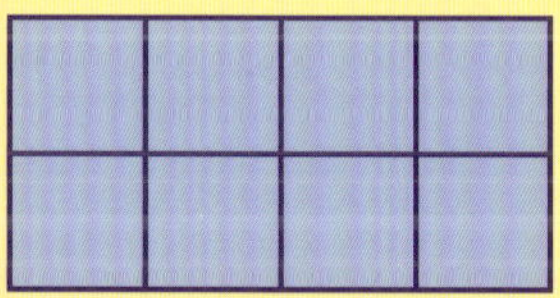

Strategy hints!

1 Look for the important words in the question.

5 Use a drawing.

9 Think logically.

ISBN 978 1 4202 9394 4

WHERE'S THE ARROW?

< < > < < >

Which of these statements describes the pattern?

- Every 2nd arrow is flipped.
- 2 arrows point right and the next one is flipped.
- 2 arrows point left and the next one is flipped.
- 2 arrows point left and the next one is turned a quarter turn right.

Extension

Where will the arrow point in these positions?

a) 30th **b)** 50th **c)** 75th **d)** 99th

Strategy hints!

1 Look for the important words in the question.

2 Look for a pattern.

5 Use a drawing.

ISBN 978 1 4202 9394 4

HOW TALL?

Lily is shorter than Katie.
Katie is taller than Reuben.
Lily is 120 centimetres tall.
Katie is 130 centimetres tall.

Which of these heights cannot be Reuben's height?

- 129 cm
- 120 cm
- 110 cm
- 135 cm

Extension

Think of 3 different people's heights and make up a height problem like this one. See if a classmate can work it out.

Strategy hints!

1 Look for the important words in the question.

5 Use a drawing.

9 Think logically.

ISBN 978 1 4202 9394 4

ANIMAL LINE-UP

Snake, Wombat, Platypus, Kangaroo and Emu are lined up in a row.
Kangaroo has 2 animals to his left and 2 animals to his right.
Wombat has no animals to her left.
Snake doesn't like his position, which is 2nd from the right.
Emu likes being next to Wombat.

List the animals as they are lined up, from left to right.

Extension

Think of 5 students in your class and make up a problem like this one. See if a classmate can work it out.

Strategy hints!

1 Look for the important words in the question.
5 Use a drawing.
9 Think logically.

ISBN 978 1 4202 9394 4

10 STICKS

Antonia uses 10 sticks and tries to make the biggest area she can.

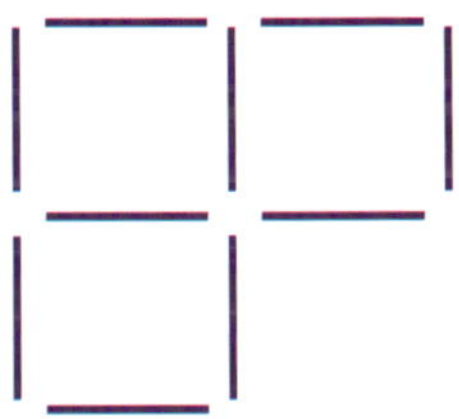

Figure out if you can make a bigger area with 10 sticks.

Extension

a) What is the biggest area you can make with 12 sticks?

b) You have 30 sticks to make the biggest square you can. How many sticks will you use?

c) How many sticks will you need to make the next possible square?

Strategy hints!

1 Look for the important words in the question.

3 Have a go.

8 Make a model.

ISBN 978 1 4202 9394 4

GOOD TIMES

What is the time 59 minutes after 4:15?

Extension

a) What is the time 59 minutes before 2:45?

b) What is the time 62 minutes after 3:59?

Strategy hints!

1 Look for the important words in the question.

5 Use a drawing.

ISBN 978 1 4202 9394 4

BUILD A BARN

Olivia builds a barn using five 3-D objects.

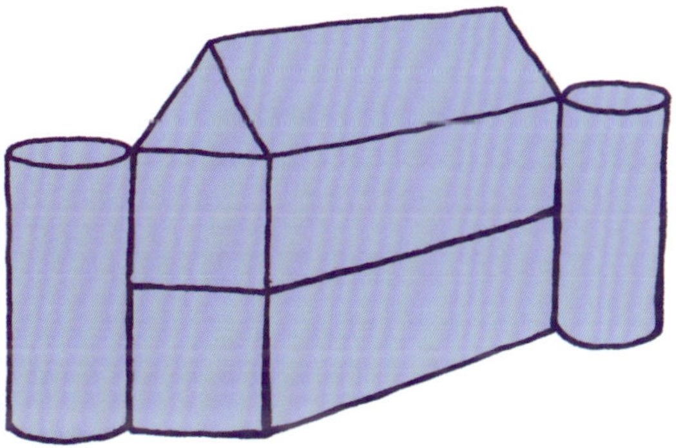

a) What five 3-D objects has Olivia used?

b) Which of these 3 different types of objects is the most common in your classroom?

Extension

How many edges altogether can be found on the five 3-D objects used to make the barn?

Strategy hints!

1 Look for the important words in the question.

5 Use a drawing.

8 Make a model.

ISBN 978 1 4202 9394 4

PAPER CUT

Toby folds a piece of paper in half and then cuts out a piece.

What will the piece of paper look like when he unfolds it?

Extension

Fold a piece of paper in half and make a cut. Predict what the paper will look like before you unfold it.

Strategy hints!

1 Look for the important words in the question.

5 Use a drawing.

8 Make a model.

ISBN 978 1 4202 9394 4

WELL BALANCED

How many triangles will balance with 4 circles?

Strategy hints!

1 Look for the important words in the question.

5 Use a drawing.

9 Think logically.

Extension

How many squares will balance with 4 circles and 3 triangles?

ISBN 978 1 4202 9394 4

LEFT, RIGHT

Wallace is walking towards a wall.
The wall is 12 forward steps away.
Instead of walking straight forwards, Wallace takes 2 steps forwards and 1 to the left.

How many times will Wallace step to the left before he reaches the wall?

Extension

Make up some problems like this one. See if a classmate can answer them.

Strategy hints!

1. Look for the important words in the question.
5. Use a drawing.
8. Make a model.

ISBN 978 1 4202 9394 4

VEGIE PATCH

Gina makes a vegie patch.
The vegie patch is a rectangle.
The distance around the patch is 20 metres.
The length of the patch is 8 metres.

How wide is the vegie patch?

Extension

Connor's vegie patch is a square.
The distance around the patch is 36 m.
What is the length of each side of Connor's vegie patch?

Strategy hints!

1. Look for the important words in the question.
5. Use a drawing.

ISBN 978 1 4202 9394 4

AMERICAN TIME

In America, they put the month before the day when they write the date.
3/7 in America means 7 March. In Australia, it means 3 July.

How many times in the year do Australians and Americans say the date the same way?

Extension

In America, how many days come between 3/4 and 4/3?

Strategy hints!

1 Look for the important words in the question.

5 Use a drawing.

ISBN 978 1 4202 9394 4

STUCK ON CUBES

Gabriel has 3 cubes. He connects 2 cubes to each other and puts the 3rd cube on top to make an 'L' shape.

a) How many square faces of the original cubes can be seen?
b) How many edges does the new shape have?
c) How many corners does the new shape have?

Extension

Gabriel wants to make a big cube out of smaller cubes. What is the least number of cubes he will need to glue together?

Strategy hints!

1 Look for the important words in the question.
5 Use a drawing.
8 Make a model.

ISBN 978 1 4202 9394 4

ARROWHEADS

In this pattern, arrowheads move in a clockwise direction and then in an anti-clockwise direction.

What will be 10th in this pattern?

Extension

What will be 20th in this pattern?

Strategy hints!

1. Look for the important words in the question.
2. Look for a pattern.
5. Use a drawing.

ISBN 978 1 4202 9394 4

BUCKET BRIGADE

Bucket A contains 9 litres of water. Bucket B is empty. Bucket C contains 3 litres of water.

Bucket A Bucket B Bucket C

Gilly wants to pour water from bucket A into buckets B and C so that they all contain the same amount of water.

How can she do this?

Extension

Will this work with 8 L of water? How about 2 L of water?

Strategy hints!

1. Look for the important words in the question.
3. Have a go.
5. Use a drawing.

ISBN 978 1 4202 9394 4

MY DESK

a) I sit in the 3rd row. I sit 2nd from the right. Which letter stands for my desk?

b) This week's lunch monitor sits in desk U. How can I get from my desk to this desk as quickly as possible without climbing over desks?

A	B	C	D	E
F	G	H	I	J
K	L	M	N	O
P	Q	R	S	T
U	V	W	X	Y

Extension

The smartest girl in the class does not sit in rows 1 or 4 or in columns 3 or 5.

In which possible seats does she sit?

Strategy hints!

1 Look for the important words in the question.

5 Use a drawing.

9 Think logically.

ISBN 978 1 4202 9394 4

AREA SQUARES

Area is often counted in squares.

Area = 1 square. 

Area = 2 squares. 

1 square is drawn using 4 lines. 2 squares are drawn using 7 lines.

How many lines are used to show an area of 3 squares?

Strategy hints!

1. Look for the important words in the question.
2. Look for a pattern.
5. Use a drawing.

Extension

What is the fewest number of lines needed to show an area of 4 squares?

ISBN 978 1 4202 9394 4

HAVE I GOT TIME?

Craig has a list of things he must do tonight.

a) What is the earliest that Craig can go to bed?

b) Can Craig play on his computer at 6:15?

c) Can Craig play cricket for an hour after doing his homework?

Must do	Start time	How long it lasts
Homework	4:00	15 minutes
Reading	5:00	1 hour
Dinner	6:30	30 minutes
Watch TV	7:00	1 hour
Brush teeth	8:15	15 minutes

Extension

a) How many minutes can Craig read before dinner, if he wants to?

b) Between 6:00 and 8:30 how much time is available for Craig to do what he wants?

Strategy hints!

1 Look for the important words in the question.

4 Use a table or a chart.

ISBN 978 1 4202 9394 4

3 CUBES

3 cubes are connected together to make a tower. The tower then stands up on a table.

How many square faces of the original cubes can be seen?

Strategy hints!

1 Look for the important words in the question.

5 Use a drawing.

8 Make a model.

Extension

The tower is now laid on its side. How many square faces of the original cubes can now be seen?

ISBN 978 1 4202 9394 4

Focus Location and transformation
- Reflection

Measurement and Geometry 24

IN A MIRROR

When letters are put in front of a mirror, they are reflected.
The right of the letter becomes the left and the left becomes the right.

Find a letter that will remain the same when reflected in a mirror. See how many you can find.

Extension

When numbers are put in front of a mirror, they are reflected. What are the first two 3-digit numbers that will remain the same when they are reflected in a mirror?

Strategy hints!

1. Look for the important words in the question.
5. Use a drawing.
9. Think logically.

ISBN 978 1 4202 9394 4

BALANCING ACT

Which one of these statements is true?

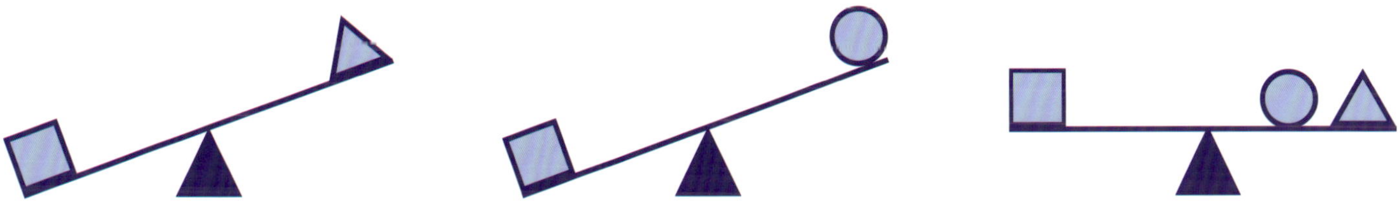

- The triangle weighs as much as the square.
- The circle is lighter than the square.
- The triangle is heavier than the circle.
- The circle and the triangle weigh the same.

Extension

Can you tell if 2 circles will be heavier than the square?

Strategy hints!

1 Look for the important words in the question.

5 Use a drawing.

9 Think logically.

ISBN 978 1 4202 9394 4

STATISTICS AND PROBABILITY

CAR COLOURS

Marcus records the colours of 12 cars that pass the post office.
He notices that they are either yellow, black or white.
He also notices that there is an equal number of cars with each colour.
The first 8 are:
Yellow, black, yellow, white, black, black, yellow, black.

What colours must the last 4 cars be?

Extension

What is the most likely colour of the 9th car?

Strategy hints!

1 Look for the important words in the question.
4 Use a table or a chart.
5 Use a drawing.

ISBN 978 1 4202 9394 4

TOWN SIZES

a) Jack lives in a town that is not the biggest or the smallest. It also does not have the biggest or the smallest population. Where might Jack live?

b) Rafael lives in a town that is bigger than at least 2 towns but has a smaller population than at least 3 towns. Where might Rafael live?

Town	Size	Population
Town A	4th	1st
Town B	2nd	3rd
Town C	3rd	5th
Town D	6th	6th
Town E	5th	2nd
Town F	1st	4th

Extension

What fraction of the towns is in the top 3 for size as well as the top 3 for population?

Strategy hints!

1 Look for the important words in the question.

4 Use a table or a chart.

ISBN 978 1 4202 9394 4

SPINNING WHEEL

Svenya buys a number for a spinning wheel at a carnival.
Her number is 84.
There are 100 numbers on the spinning wheel.
The number that won last time was 84.

Is 84 the best number to get?

Extension

What is Svenya's chance of winning the spin?

Strategy hints!

1 Look for the important words in the question.

5 Use a drawing.

9 Think logically.

ISBN 978 1 4202 9394 4

TEACHERS' SHOES

a) Each teacher wants to wear shoes that are the same colour as their name. Which teachers should swap shoes to make this possible?

b) What is the smallest number of swaps needed if each teacher wants to wear a different colour shoe to their name?

Teacher	Shoe colour
Mr Grey	white
Mrs Brown	brown
Mr Black	black
Ms Green	green
Mr White	grey

Extension

In the order on the list, each teacher has twice as many pairs of shoes as the teacher before them. Mr Grey has 3 pairs of shoes. Who has 24 pairs of shoes?

Strategy hints!

1 Look for the important words in the question.

4 Use a table or a chart.

9 Think logically.

ISBN 978 1 4202 9394 4

CARD CHANCE

10 cards numbered 1 to 10 are put into a hat.
1 card is taken out.

Which of these has the best chance of happening?

- The card is an even number.
- The card is 7 or higher.
- The card is 4 or smaller.
- The card is a number starting with the letter 'T'.

Extension

What are the chances out of 10 for each of these 4 possible results?

Strategy hints!

1 Look for the important words in the question.

9 Think logically.

ISBN 978 1 4202 9394 4

DICE ROLL

Luka rolls a die and records the numbers he rolls.

Number rolled	Number of rolls
1	2
2	4
3	1
4	5
5	3
6	3

a) How many times does Luka roll the die?

b) What is the difference between the most amount of times a number was rolled and the least amount of times a number was rolled?

c) How many more times did Luka roll an even number than an odd number?

d) How many times did Luka roll a number less than 4?

Strategy hints!

1 Look for the important words in the question.

4 Use a table or a chart.

9 Think logically.

Extension

Is 4 the easiest number to roll with a die?

ISBN 978 1 4202 9394 4

COIN PATTERN

Raza tosses a coin 6 times and sees that the results are:

Heads, tails, heads, tails, heads, tails.

Raza tosses his coin another 6 times and gets more heads than tails.

If you include all 12 coin tosses, what is the total number of heads and tails that Raza could have tossed?

Extension

If you toss a coin 3 times there are 8 possible results.
List the 8 possible results.

Strategy hints!

1 Look for the important words in the question.

9 Think logically.

ISBN 978 1 4202 9394 4

TV SETS

Year 2 was asked about the number of TV sets they have at home. The results were recorded in a table.

TV sets	Homes
0	1
1	4
2	8
3	3
4	2
More than 4	2

a) How many students' homes were in the survey?
b) How many homes had more than 2 TV sets?
c) How many homes had fewer than 3 TVs?

Extension

There were 48 TVs in the survey.

How many TVs must the homes have had that were in the 'More than 4' section?

Strategy hints!

1 Look for the important words in the question.
4 Use a table or a chart.
9 Think logically.

ISBN 978 1 4202 9394 4

TEDDY PICK

In a bag there are 2 red, 2 green and 2 yellow teddies.

How many do you need to take out of the bag to be sure of picking a red teddy?

Extension

Amy picks a red teddy, then a green teddy, then a yellow teddy.
What is the chance that the next teddy will not be red?

Strategy hints!

1. Look for the important words in the question.
4. Use a table or a chart.
9. Think logically.

ISBN 978 1 4202 9394 4

6 APPLES

6 apples of exactly the same size are in a bag.
3 are green and 3 are red.
Patrick wants to pick out 1 green apple.

What is the smallest number of apples Patrick needs to pick from the bag to have a chance of picking a green apple?

Extension

What is the smallest number of apples Patrick needs to pick from the bag to be sure of picking a green apple?

Strategy hints!

1 Look for the important words in the question.
7 Try an easier problem.
8 Make a model.

ISBN 978 1 4202 9394 4

ANSWERS

Number and Algebra

Answers 1

1. **Code cracker**: **a)** 497; **b)** 5475; **c)** 1981185
(Hint: The letter value is its place in the alphabet.)
Extension: 10 (There are 10 years in a decade.)

2. **Letter shift**: **a)** Frog; **b)** Jessica; **c)** Twelve
(Hint: The letters have been moved forwards by 1 letter in the alphabet.)
Extension: Answers will vary.

3. **Letter pattern**: **a)** I; **b)** M, S; **c)** 13 letters. The last letter will be Y.
(Hint: The pattern misses every 2nd letter.)
Extension: Answers will vary.

4. **Symbol shocker**: **a)** [*] means put the 2 numbers together and then take away 2; **b)** 85
Extension: $31 + 15 = 46$

5. **Read the signs**: **a)** [^] means take away and [#] means add; **b)** 40
Extension: Answers will vary.

6. **Calculator slip**: $100 + 10 - 20 + 5$
(Hint: Take away the biggest number to get an answer less than 100.)
Extension: $100 - 10 - 20 + 5$

7. **Wrong number**: $10 \times 10 - 10 + 1$
(Hint: The large answer of 91 means that multiplication must have been used.)
Extension: **a)** $5 \times 2 + 2 - 1$; **b)** $3 + 5 - 2 + 3$

8. **Boxed in**: $4 \times 5 + 6 - 7$ or $5 \times 4 + 6 - 7$
Extension: **a)** $10 - 8 \times 5 \times 2$ or $10 - 8 \times 2 \times 5$
b) $5 \times 4 \times 3 - 10$ or $5 \times 3 \times 4 - 10$

9. **Boxed up**: $20 \times 3 - 5$ or $30 \times 2 - 5$
Extension: $(57 - 6) \times 2 = 102$

10. **Coin count**: 5 answers
1: $\$1 + 20c + 5c + 5c + 5c + 5c$
2: $\$1 + 10c + 10c + 10c + 5c + 5c$
3: $50c + 50c + 20c + 10c + 5c + 5c$
4: $50c + 50c + 10c + 10c + 10c + 10c$
5: $50c + 20c + 20c + 20c + 20c + 10c$
(Hint: Start with the most expensive coin possible.)
Extension: 3 answers
1: $\$1 + 20c + 20c + 20c$
2: $\$1 + 50c + 5c + 5c$
3: $50c + 50c + 50c + 10c$

ISBN 978 1 4202 9394 4

Number and Algebra

Answers 2

11. **Light bar logic**: 1, 2, 3, 4, 5, 7, 11
(Hint: Use digits that use a small number of light bars.)
Extension: 21, 24, 27, 31, 34, 37, 41, 42, 43, 44, 45, 47

12. **Light lesson**: 14 light bars. 243, 324, 342, 423 and 432
Extension: 808, 868, 880, 886, 889, 898, 988

13. **Lighten up**: 51
(Hint: No numbers on a calculator use 3 light bars.)
Extension: 8, 12, 13, 15, 21, 31 and 51

14. **Giraffes and pandas**: **a)** Giraffe $7; **b)** Panda $6
(Hint: Divide $14 by 2.)
Extension: **a)** $3; **b)** $70

15. **Footballs and cricket bats**: $14
(Hint: Football $8, bat $6)
Extension: **a)** $34; **b)** $76

16. **Shoes and socks**: $10
(Hint: $30 is 3 times as much as $10.)
Extension: **a)** No, total cost is $110; **b)** Yes, total cost is $90

17. **Hats and gloves**: 90 cents
(Hint: $1.10 – 90 cents = 20 cents)
Extension: Answers will vary.

18. **Goldfish and seahorses**: $10
(Hint: 1 goldfish must cost $3.
$10 + $3 + $3 + $3 + $3 + $3 = $25)
Extension: $2

19. **Grand sale**: $19
(Hint: On sale, books cost $5 and pens $2.)
Extension: **a)** Yes, total cost is $35 with $5 change; **b)** No, total cost is $54

20. **What number am I?**: 898
(Hint: 8 is half of 16.)
Extension: Answers will vary.

21. **Name my number**: 172 or 190
(Hint: 1 is the only digit that uses 2 light bars.)
Extension: 415 or 433

ISBN 978 1 4202 9394 4

Answers 3

22. **Number me**: 345
(Hint: The number is odd, so it must end in 5.)
Extension: Answers will vary.

23. **Know my number**: **a)** 470, 472, 474, 476, 478; **b)** 478
(Hint: The number must be in the 470s and even.)
Extension: Answers will vary.

24. **Number quiz**: 284, 464, 482
Extension: 365, 383, 563, 185, 581

25. **India's money**: \$3.05
(Hint: 20c + 20c + 50c + \$1 + \$1 + 5c + 5c + 5c = \$3.05)
Extension: Answers will vary.

26. **All in a line**: 20
(Hint: Don't forget to count Brian's partner.)
Extension: 24 girls, 16 boys

27. **Class line**: 11 students
(Hint: There must be 5 students in front and 5 students behind Emma.)
Extension: 8 boys

28. **Easter egg hunt**: 11 eggs
(Hint: Add them all up and split them into 3 equal parts.)
Extension: **a)** No, 26 eggs won't divide into 3 equal parts; **b)** Yes, 66 will divide into 3 equal parts.

29. **Ali, Sam and Ben**: Ben, Sam, Ali
(Hint: Sam's age doesn't matter.)
Extension: **a)** Yes. Both Ben and Sam could be 11 years old and Ben still be older. **b)** Answers will vary.

30. **Equal Street**: 7 houses
(Hint: 28 = 7 groups of 4.)
Extension: 33 more windows

31. **Farmer Joe**: 5 pens
(Hint: Split 10 into 5 groups of 2.)
Extension: **a)** 24 pigs and 60 chickens; **b)** 30 pigs and 75 chickens; **c)** 40 pigs and 100 chickens

32. **How many numbers?**: 6 numbers: 100, 110, 120, 130, 140, 150
(Hint: They must end in zero.)
Extension: 61

ISBN 978 1 4202 9394 4

33. **Sticker time**: 11 stickers
(Hint: The answer must be 1 more than the 10 times table.)
Extension: 55 stamps

34. **Straight as an arrow**: 3, 7, 7, 10
(Hint: The order does not matter.)
Extension: **a)** 0, 7, 10, 10; **b)** 0, 10 or 3, 7

35. **Tens and ones**: 19, 28, 37, 46, 55, 64, 73, 82, 91
(Hint: Change the 10s and 1s places to find another answer.)
Extension: 17, 28, 39, 60, 71, 82, 93

36. **Digit sum**: 159, 168, 177, 186, 195
(Hint: Change the 10s and 1s places to find another answer.)
Extension: 249, 258, 267, 276, 285, 294

37. **All the twos**: 20
(Hint: 22 has two 2s.)
Extension: 100

38. **All the digits**: 192 digits
(Hint: There are 90 2-digit numbers.)
Extension: 300 digits

39. **Slippery stairs**: 14th step
(Hint: Start at the end and then move to the start of the problem.)
Extension: Answers will vary.

40. **Snakes and adders**: 39
(Hint: 37 + 20 – 8 – 10 = 39)
Extension: 6 ways

1: 1 + 6	4: 4 + 3
2: 2 + 5	5: 5 + 2
3: 3 + 4	6: 6 + 1

41. **Going halves**: $20
(Hint: If Milo gave half of his money to Greg, he must have $40 left as well.)
Extension: Answers will vary.

42. **Which column?**: G
(Hint: Each column adds on 7 to the number above it.)
Extension: Column B, the 7 times table

ISBN 978 1 4202 9394 4

43. **Counting columns**: A
(Hint: It is the 9s counting pattern.)
Extension: B

44. **Odd one out**: **a)** 35; **b)** It is the only number whose digits do not add up to 9.
Extension: 24. All other numbers are shown on the calculator by 6 light bars.

45. **Not like the others**: **a)** 479; **b)** The only number where the digits do not get smaller from left to right.
Extension: 714. The digits of all the other numbers add up to 11.

46. **All the coins**: You will have 15 cents more.
(Hint: All the silver coins add up to 85 cents.)
Extension: $1.15

47. **Magic square**

16	2	12
6	10	14
8	18	4

Extension: There are many answers that work, but will all have 10 in the centre.

48. **All about the place**: 247, 274, 427, 472, 724, 742
(Hint: Put the digits in number order.)
Extension: 358, 385, 538, 583, 835, 853

49. **Perfect placement**: 244, 424, 442
(Hint: The smallest number moves to the right as the numbers grow in size.)
Extension: **a)** 224, 242, 244, 422, 424, 442;
b) 6 answers: 4466, 4646, 4664, 6446, 6464, 6644

50. **Making numbers**: 5163
Extension: 2936

51. **My town**: 4959
Extension: Answers will vary.

52. **Letterboxes**: 13 houses
(Hint: Count the odd numbers, stopping at 25.)
Extension: 30 houses

ISBN 978 1 4202 9394 4

53. **Street knowledge**: 40 or 41
(Hint: The numbers must follow on from each other.)
Extension: 5 houses

54. **Letter sale**: Answers will vary.
Extension: Answers will vary.

55. **Sign sale**: Answers will vary.
Extension: **a)** 3 vowels, 4 consonants; **b)** 3 vowels, 5 consonants

56. **Back to back**: 5, 6 and 7
(Hint: 3 groups of 6 equals 18.)
Extension: **a)** 11, 12 and 13; **b)** 29, 30, 31

57. **Consecutive challenge**: 10
(Hint: The middle number must be 9.)
Extension: **a)** 20; **b)** 19

58. **Temperature times**: 29 degrees
(Hint: 27 – 4 then 27 – 21)
Extension: 8 degrees (26 – 4 = 22; 26 – 8 = 18)

59. **All sorts of sums**: **a)** 20 + 12; **b)** 20 – 12
(Hint: Try many possible combinations.)
Extension: **a)** 2 + 0 – 1 + 2 or 2 x 0 + 1 + 2; **b)** 20 – 1 + 2

60. **Equal coins**: 20
(Hint: 20 x 5 cents = 100 cents, or $1)
Extension: **a)** 5; **b)** Answers will vary.

61. **So many sums**: **a)** 23 + 5; **b)** 2 + 3 + 5
(Hint: Try many possible combinations.)
Extension: **a)** 53 – 2; **b)** 25 – 3

62. **In a bracket**: **a)** 50; **b)** 24; **c)** 60
(Hint: Remember to do what is inside the bracket first.)
Extension: Answers will vary.

63. **Mice and men**: 30 legs
(Hint: Mice = 20 legs, Men = 10 legs)
Extension: Answers will vary.

64. **Bicycles and tricycles**: 3 tricycles
(Hint: 3 x 3 + 8 x 2 = 25)
Extension: Answers will vary.

65. **Birthday money**: $32
(Hint: The doubling pattern is 1, 2, 4, 8, 16, 32 . . .)
Extension: **a)** On her 9th birthday; **b)** $512

ISBN 978 1 4202 9394 4

66. Aussie rules: 4 ways
1: 3 goals + 2 behinds
2: 2 goals + 8 behinds
3: 1 goal + 14 behinds
4: 0 goals + 20 behinds
(Hint: 6 + 6 + 6 + 2 = 20)
Extension: 4 goals + 3 behinds

67. Rugby rules: 3 ways
1: 2 tries + 1 penalty
2: 1 try + 3 penalties
3: 5 penalties
(Hint: 4 + 4 + 2 = 10)
Extension: 5 tries + 5 penalties

68. Follow the symbols: 38
(Hint: 14 – 4 = 10; 10 x 2 = 20; 20 x 2 = 40; 40 + 2 = 42; 42 – 4 = 38)
Extension: 20

69. Biggest number: **a)** 13; **b)** 38
Extension: 35, 10, 10, 10

70. Leftovers: 11
(Hint: 100 – 11 – 8 = 81; 81 – 70 = 11)
Extension: 56

71. Ed and Evie: 18
(Hint: 14 + 18 = 32 and 18 – 14 = 4)
Extension: 36 years

72. Nanny and Grandad: 135
(Hint: 70 + 65)
Extension: 1945

73. Lucy and Lou: 11
(Hint: Lou tells the truth.)
Extension: Answers will vary.

74. Planet Zebko: **a)** 17; **b)** 16; **c)** 56
(Hint: Add up each symbol one at a time.)
Extension: 125

75. Alien maths test: **a)** 22; **b)** 14; **c)** 100
(Hint: 7 + 15, 20 – 6, 50 x 2)
Extension: Answers will vary.

76. 10 times smaller: 23
(Hint: 20 + 4 – 3 + 2)
Extension: **a)** 1; **b)** $\frac{1}{2}$; **c)** $\frac{1}{10}$

ISBN 978 1 4202 9394 4

77. Pick the pattern: **a)** The numbers are halving or being divided by 2; **b)** 16; **c)** $\frac{1}{2}$, $\frac{1}{4}$; **d)** $\frac{1}{8}$
(Hint: This pattern will never end.)
Extension: 7 numbers before 1

78. Jack, queen, king: 3 ways
1: 5 queens
2: 1 king + 3 queens + 1 jack
3: 2 kings + 1 queen + 2 jacks
(Hint: Think of all the different ways to add up to 10 using 3, 2 and 1.)
Extension: 4 kings

79. Abbey, Bert and Cindi: 6 ways: ABC, ACB, BAC, BCA, CAB, CBA
(Hint: Each student can have 2 different students behind them.)
Extension: 24 ways

80. Doors and windows: 4 different ways
1: Red + Yellow
2: Red + Red
3: Yellow + Red
4: Yellow + Yellow
Extension: 9 different ways
1: Red + Yellow
2: Red + Red
3: Yellow + Red
4: Yellow + Yellow
5: Green + Yellow
6: Green + Red
7: Green + Green
8: Yellow + Green
9: Red + Green

81. Finals time: 3 rounds of matches

Round 1	Jets v. Cheetahs	Doves v. Kings
Round 2	Kings v. Cheetahs	Jets v. Doves
Round 3	Jets v. Kings	Doves v. Cheetahs

Extension: 2 matches

ISBN 978 1 4202 9394 4

82. Palindrome puzzle: **a)** 11; **b)** 99; **c)** 101; **d)** 999
(Hint: Use either the biggest or smallest possible digits in your answers.)
Extension: **a)** 111; **b)** 989; **c)** 323, 424, 525, 626, 727, 828, 929; **d)** 202, 212, 232, 242, 252, 262, 272, 282, 292

83. Back to front: 22 + 77, 33 + 66 and 44 + 55
(Hint: Look for a pattern in the answers.)
Extension: 22 + 99, 33 + 88, 44 + 77 and 55 + 66

84. Time is money: $12
(Hint: She worked 6 lots of 15 minutes.)
Extension **a)** 4:45; **b)** $44, only $6 away from $50

85. Not 2 or 5: 8
(Hint: 1, 3, 7, 9, 11, 13, 17, 19)
Extension: 20

86. Shopping: $38
(Hint: $7 + $7 + $4 + $4 + $4 + $5 + $7 = $38)
Extension: Answers will vary.

87. 2 away: 8, 10 and 12
(Hint: The middle number must be 30 divided by 3.)
Extension: 20, 22, 24

88. Our towns: 18 km
(Hint: 18 is half of 36.)
Extension: 27 km

89. Counting in fives: 53, 78, 418
(Hint: All answers will end in either 3 or 8.)
Extension: 993 and 998

90. Race place: 10 boys
(Hint: I finished 4th.)
Extension: Clare, Eve, Amy, Danni, Fiona, Beth

91. Make that number: **a)** 1 + 2 + 3 + 4 – 5;
b) 12 – 3 – 4 + 5
(Hint: Are these the only answers that work?)
Extension: **a)** 1 + 23 + 4 – 5;
b) 1 + 2 – 3 + 45 or 12 x 3 + 4 + 5

ISBN 978 1 4202 9394 4

92. Marbles: **a)** Grace gets 4 marbles, Tate gets 3 marbles; **b)** 5 marbles are left in the bag.
(Hint: There were 12 in the bag.)
Extension: 36 marbles

93. Calculator correction: **a)** 5; **b)** Type [+] [5] [=] to get 14
(Hint: 14 – 9 = 5)
Extension: **a)** Type [–] [6] [=] to get 8;
b) Type [+] [55] [=] to get 68

94. An open book: Pages 62 and 63
(Hint: Try with a 4 page book.)
Extension: 93 pages

95. Booked out: An odd number
Extension: 64 pages

96. Animal sizes: 8 mice
(Hint: 2 x 2 x 2)
Extension: $\frac{1}{8}$

97. Odd or even: 10
(Hint: All the odd numbers in the 10s and all the even numbers in the 20s.)
Extension: **a)** 11; **b)** 11; **c)** 10

98. Buying stamps: 10 stamps
(Hint: 10 x 3 cents + 2 x 5 cents = 40 cents and 12 stamps)
Extension: 6

99. Starting number: 21
(Hint: 24 + 2 – 5)
Extension: 9 (9 + 5 + 4 ÷ 2 = 9)

100. Tennis anyone?: 3 ways
1: AB v. CD
2: AC v. BD
3: AD v. BC
Extension: 6 ways
1: A v. B
2: A v. C
3: A v. D
4: B v. C
5: B v. D
6: C v. D

ISBN 978 1 4202 9394 4

1. **The Bear family**: 2 baby bears
   (Hint: 3 mammas must weigh the same as 6 baby bears.)
   Extension: 5 baby bears

2. **SUM**:

S	M	U
M	U	S
U	S	M

   (Hint: The same letter must appear 3 times in a diagonal line)
   Extension: More than one answer is possible.

T	N	E
N	E	T
E	T	N

3. **Fill in the space**: 16 rectangles
   (Hint: 60 – 16 = 44)
   Extension: 2 colours

4. **Amazing date**: 22/8/30, 21/9/30, 20/10/30, 19/11/30, 18/12/30
   (Hint: The days decrease by 1 as the months go up by 1.)
   Extension: 31/12/43

5. **All the squares**: 14 squares
   (Hint: 9 single squares + 4 squares made up of 4 smaller squares + the whole shape is a square)
   Extension: 11 squares

6. **Where's the arrow?**: 2 arrows point left and the next one is flipped.
   (Hint: All arrows in the 3 times table, like the 30th, will point right.)
   Extension **a)** >; **b)** <; **c)** >; **d)** >

7. **How tall?**: 135 cm
   (Hint: All others can be true.)
   Extension: Answers will vary.

8. **Animal line-up**: Wombat, Emu, Kangaroo, Snake, Platypus
   Extension: Answers will vary.

ISBN 978 1 4202 9394 4

9. **10 sticks**:
(Hint: The biggest area will take up the most space. Other options are possible.)

Extension:
a)

b) 28 (7 sticks on each side);
c) 32 (8 sticks on each side)

10. **Good times**: 5:14
(Hint: 59 minutes is 1 minute less than 1 hour.)
Extension: **a)** 1:46; **b)** 5:01

11. **Build a barn**: **a)** 2 cylinders + 2 rectangular prisms + 1 triangular prism; **b)** Probably rectangular prisms, but answers may vary.
(Hint: Look for bricks, cupboards, books. They are all rectangular prisms.)
Extension: 37 (cylinder has 2 edges, rectangular prism has 12 edges, triangular prism has 9 edges)

12. **Paper cut**:

(Hint: This is like a mirror image)
Extension: Answers will vary.

13. **Well balanced**: 6 triangles
(Hint: 2 lots of 3)
Extension: 3 squares

14. **Left, right**: 5 times
(Hint: After 12 steps he will reach the wall and not need another step to the left.)
Extension: Answers will vary.

15. **Vegie patch**: 2 m
(Hint: 8 + 2 + 8 + 2 = 20)
Extension: 9 m

16. **American time**: 12
(Hint: When the day and the month have the same number.)
Extension: 30 days

ISBN 978 1 4202 9394 4

17. **Stuck on cubes**: **a)** 14; **b)** 18; **c)** 12
Extension: 8 cubes

18. **Arrowheads**: ←
(Hint: This arrow will come in position 4, 10, 16, 22 . . .)
Extension: →

19. **Bucket brigade**: Pour 4 L into B and 1 L into C so that all have 4 L of water.
Extension: No. The numbers altogether must be in the 3 times table.

20. **My desk**: **a)** Desk N; **b)** Go left to desk K and then down to desk U.
Extension: 9 seats: F, G, I, K, L, N, U, V, X

21. **Area squares**: 10 lines
Extension: 12 lines
(Hint: Use a 2 x 2 square.)

22. **Have I got time? a)** 8:30; **b)** Yes; **c)** No
(Hint: He is free from 6:00 to 6:30.)
Extension: **a)** 2 hours and 15 minutes;
b) 45 minutes, or 1 hour and 45 minutes if TV is considered free time.

23. **3 cubes**: 13
(Hint: 3 squares are visible on 4 sides of the tower plus 1 on top.)
Extension: 11

24. **In a mirror**: A, H, I, M, O, T, U, V, W, X, Y
(Hint: These letters are symmetrical top to bottom.)
Extension: 101, 111

25. **Balancing act**: The circle is lighter than the square.
(Hint: There is not enough information to tell if the other answers are true.)
Extension: No, you can't tell.

ISBN 978 1 4202 9394 4

Statistics and Probability

Answers 14

1. **Car colours**: 3 white and 1 yellow
(Hint: There were 4 of each colour.)
Extension: White is the most likely.

2. **Town sizes**: **a)** Town B, Town C or Town E;
b) Town C or Town F
(Hint: The table removes Town F and Town D for size and Town A and Town D for population.)
Extension: $\frac{1}{6}$

3. **Spinning wheel**: It has the same chance as any other number.
(Hint: The spin is different each time.)
Extension: 1 chance in 100

4. **Teachers' shoes**: **a)** Mr Grey and Mr White should swap shoes; **b)** 2 swaps
(Hint: Each swap will change 2 teachers at a time.)
Extension: Ms Green

5. **Card chance**: The card is an even number.
(Hint: 5 cards are even.)
Extension: **a)** 5 chances in 10; **b)** 4 chances in 10; **c)** 4 chances in 10; **d)** 3 chances in 10

6. **Dice roll**: **a)** 18; **b)** 4; **c)** 6 times; **d)** 7 times
Extension: No
(Hint: All 6 numbers have the same chance of being rolled.)

7. **Coin pattern**:
1: 9 heads + 3 tails
2: 8 heads + 4 tails
3: 7 heads + 5 tails
(Hint: The sum must be 12 and heads must be more than 6.)
Extension:
1: Tails + tails + tails
2: Tails + tails + heads
3: Tails + heads + heads
4: Tails + heads + tails
5: Heads + heads + heads
6: Heads + heads + tails
7: Heads + tails + tails
8: Heads + tails + heads

ISBN 978 1 4202 9394 4

8. **TV sets**: **a)** 20 homes; **b)** 7 homes **c)** 13 homes
   Extension: 5 and 6
9. **Teddy pick**: 5
   (Hint: The first 4 could be 2 green and 2 yellow.)
   Extension: 2 out of 3
10. **6 apples**: 1 apple
    Extension: 4 apples
    (Hint: The first 3 might all be red.)

ISBN 978 1 4202 9394 4

CD

Contents

User Agreement

The material on this disk is copyrighted.

The individual purchaser, or purchasing school or institution, may:

- use the PDFs on unlimited computers by installing them on a single secure network server for access from one site, or on multiple computers for access from one geographical site.
- Problem Solving Card PDFs on the CD are not printable. They may be viewed on IWBs or similar within the purchasing educational institution. Other content on the CD may be reproduced in accordance with the Australian *Copyright Act 1968* (the Act) and provided the educational institution (or body that administers it) has given a remuneration notice to the Copyright Agency Limited (CAL) under the Act.

You may not:

- copy for, transmit to, or allow use by the staff of a non-purchasing school or institution.
- sell the product or copies to another person or institution.
- sell any modified or adapted files from the CD-ROM or allow them to be transmitted or sold to another individual or educational institution.
- remove or alter any copyright notice or other proprietary notice or label.

Unauthorised copying is prohibited. Both individuals and institutions are liable for large fines for breaking copyright laws. Thank you for your cooperation.